IMAGES
of Aviation

AIRSHIPS
OF THE
FIRST WORLD WAR

His Majesty's Aiship No.1, or *Mayfly*, as she was known, after the accident of 1911 in which her back was broken.

IMAGES
of Aviation

AIRSHIPS
OF THE
FIRST WORLD WAR

Compiled by
Terry C. Treadwell and Alan C. Wood

TEMPUS

First published 1999
Copyright © Terry C. Treadwell and Alan C. Wood, 1999

Tempus Publishing Limited
The Mill, Brimscombe Port,
Stroud, Gloucestershire, GL5 2QG

ISBN 0 7524 1629 4

Typesetting and origination by
Tempus Publishing Limited
Printed in Great Britain by
Midway Clark Printing, Wiltshire

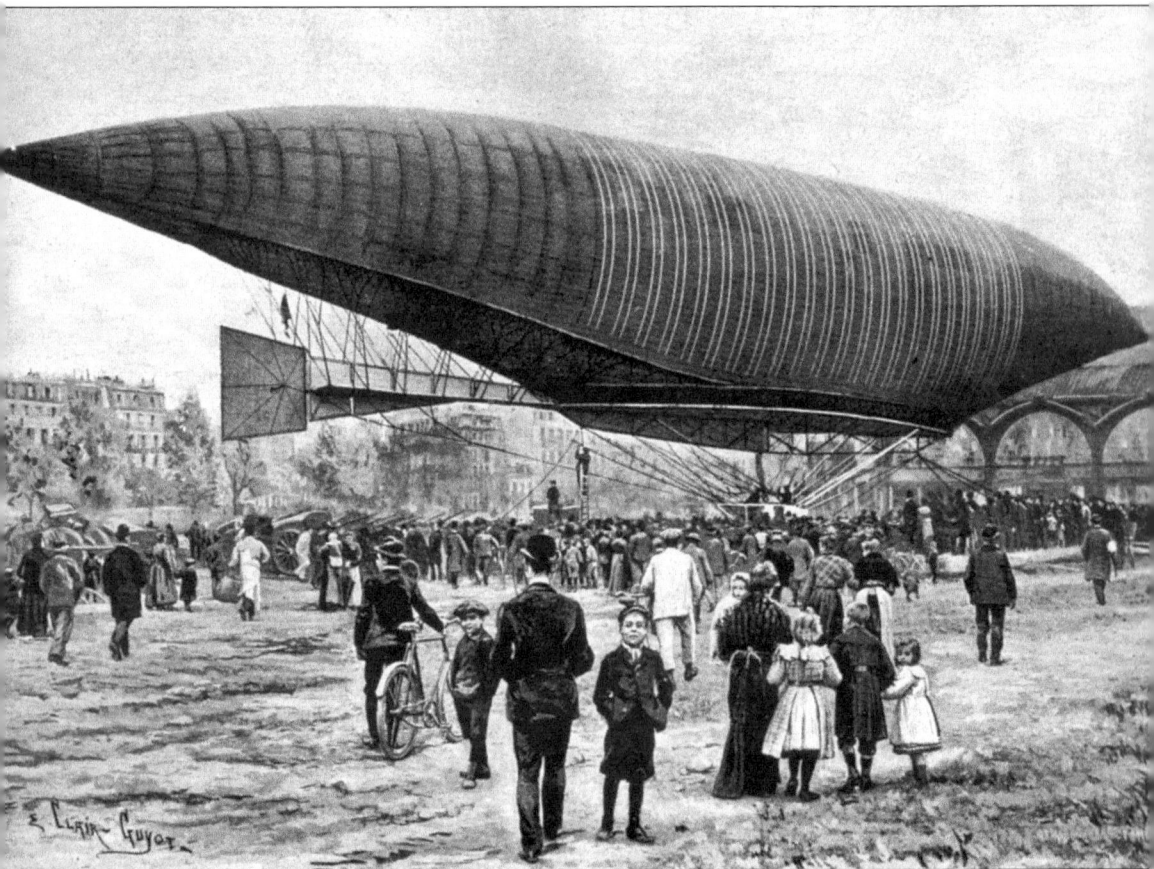

Crowds gather to watch a flight of the French dirigible *Lebaudy* in 1903.

Contents

An engraving by Havell of E.M. Jones' drawing celebrating the achievemnts of Mr Sadler, an early British aeronaut shown here ascending over Oxford.

Introduction

Although the theory of flight goes back into the depths of history, the story of the balloon and the airship only goes back a couple of hundred years or so. The first recorded manned flight in a balloon was on 15 October 1783, when a Frenchman, Pilâtre de Rozier, ascended from Paris in a Montgolfier-built, tethered hot air balloon to the great height of 84ft. One month later de Rozier, this time accompanied by the Marquess d'Arlandes, took to the air in an untethered flight over Paris. The balloon rose to a height of 3000ft, coming down some five miles from its starting point. Paris rapidly becameg the centre of world flying and was invaded by aeronauts from different countries around the world.

During the Franco-Prussian War of 1870-1871, two balloon companies of *aérostiers* were formed under the command of Captain Coutelle. The first recorded operational flight, however, was made on 2 June 1794, when Coutelle made an ascent from Maubeuge to observe the disposition of the Austrian and Dutch troops. His balloon, *L'Entreprenant*, was moved to Fleurus where, during the battle, he and his balloon stayed aloft for over ten hours, directing the French artillery. For his part in the action, Coutelle was given command of the Balloon Corps, which now consisted of four companies. During the Siege of Paris, Jules Durof's balloon, *Neptune*, was used by Félix Tournachon (aka 'Nadar') as an observation platform. The balloon was launched from the Place Saint Pierre in Montmartre and was used to supply troop movements to General Trochu, who was in charge of the defence of Paris.

There were a number of balloon flights during the next hundred years. The first airship flight was by a French airship, *La France*, on 9 August 1884, flown by Captain Charles Renard and Arthur Krebs. It was the first powered flight of any LTA (lighter-than-air) craft. Built at Chalais-Meudon, *La France* was powered by an electric motor, enabling the airship to reach a speed of 15mph, and was the first to be able to make a circular flight, as opposed to the early balloons which were at the mercy of the prevailing winds.

It is at this point that the terms 'rigid' and 'non-rigid', although relatively self-explanatory, may require some more detailed explanation. A rigid airship retains its shape because it is designed and built with a framework of either metal or wood, with bags containing the gas held within it and a skin over the top of the framework. The non-rigid airship has no framework and retains its unsupported shape due to the construction of the outer skin and the pressure of the gas inside the shaped envelope. There was later a semi-rigid construction which had a central spine or keel made of metal or wood to which the engines and control areas were fixed. The keel also helped retain the shape of the outer envelope.

It wasn't until 2 July 1900 that the first airship powered by a combustion engine took to the air. The *Luftschiff Zeppelin I* (LZ.I) built by Count Ferdinand von Zeppelin and, it is said, designed by Professor Müller-Breslau, made its first flight over Lake Constance. The LZ.I made a total of three flights totalling three hours before being scrapped. Among a number of other defects it was found to be seriously under-powered. Lessons had been learned, however, and further Zeppelins were built with some success. The 'LZ' identification mark was one allocated by the builders and used by the army but was shortened to just 'L' when the airships were used by the German Navy.

Back in Paris, on 19 October 1901, a Brazilian inventor by the name of Alberto Santos-Dumont flew his dirigible airship, powered by a 12hp engine, around the Eiffel Tower at a speed of 15mph. During a period between 1898 and 1907, Santos-Dumont built and flew a total of sixteen airships, but although relatively successful he never achieved the recognition he strove for and died in relative obscurity in 1932 without reaching any of his goals.

The First World War heralded the arrival of the first practical airships, necessity being the mother of invention. As an engineering officer in the German Army, Count von Zeppelin had been sent to the United States as an observer and seen the effects of using observation balloons in the American Civil War. He realised the potential of the airship in battle. With the relative failure of the LZ.I in 1900, von Zeppelin got to work building the LZ.2, this time with two engines. After a number of teething troubles the actual flight was a success, but ended in disaster when one of the engines failed. These flights were witnessed by a journalist by the name of Hugo Eckener, who was later to become an integral part of the Zeppelin organisation.

Up to this point all of von Zeppelin's financing had come from private sources, but with

An early Zeppelin on trials over Lake Constance.

the arrival of the LZ.3, the German government started to take a closer interest in the rigid airship and awarded the company 500,000 marks for further development work. Within months the government had placed two orders for airships at a cost of over 1,000,000 marks each. The first, the LZ.3, had already proved itself during trials, while the second of the two ordered was the LZ.4. The flights of the LZ.4 were an unqualified success, so much so that the King and Queen of Württemberg were two of its earliest passengers. This was the first time that members of any royal family had ever flown and in effect gave the royal seal of approval to the airship.

On 4 August 1908 the LZ.4 took off on a 24-hour test flight. On board were Count von Zeppelin and ten others. The flight went well until one of the engines failed. After emergency repairs the flight continued, but the airship broke down again. This time von Zeppelin managed to get the airship to Daimler's plant for them to make the repairs to the engine. Unfortunately, as they approached the ground, soldiers took hold of the mooring lines and, because of their inexperience in handling such a craft, mishandled the airship, causing it to crash into the ground and catch fire. The mangled mess of wreckage would have spelt disaster for most men, but it seemed to inspire the now seventy-year-old von Zeppelin. The government, realising that there was a future in airships, pushed von Zeppelin on financially, helping him create the Deutsche Luftschiffahrts-Aktien-Gesellschaft (DELAG).

The only airship von Zeppelin had left was the LZ.3, which was in the process of being refurbished, but the army wanted to have their own airship and took over the LZ.3 before the tests were completed. The count then produced the next airship for the army, LZ.5. Again, bad luck dogged von Zeppelin and during tests it too crashed. Quickly repaired, it

Count von Zeppelin on board LZ.30 on 28 May 1916. The officer with him is Hauptmann Macher, captain of the airship.

Zeppelin L.31, with her distinctive Iron Cross marking.

was handed over to the army for tests, but during a bad landing in high winds it was ripped apart and totally destroyed.

The next airship, LZ.6, was without doubt one of the best. Most of the problems that beset the earlier airships had been ironed out and during one cross-country trip, on 25 August 1909, the craft carried Count von Zeppelin, a number of government officials and one very distinguished passenger – Orville Wright. It would have been interesting to have eavesdropped on the conversation between the two major exponents of the heavier-than-air and the lighter-than-air craft of that time, but unfortunately no record exists of the conversation between them.

The first German naval Zeppelin, L.1 (LZ.14), was completed in 1912, but crashed less than six months later in the North Sea on 9 September 1913, killing the head of the Naval Airship Division, Korvettenkapitän Friedrich Metzing. The second naval Zeppelin, L.2, did not fare much better. It was lost when it caught fire during altitude tests on its tenth flight. There were no survivors. These disasters undermined Grand Admiral von Tirpitz's faith in the airship and he appointed Korvettenkapitän Peter Strasser to take over as head of the Naval Airship Division. Strasser set about trying to build the Airship Division back up and persuaded von Tirpitz that the unit needed another airship. With great reluctance von Tirpitz ordered a third Zeppelin, the L.3, so that the Airship Division could at least have one airship on which to train.

Zeppelin was not alone in German airship manufacturing. Another company, the Luftschiffbau Schütte-Lanz, founded in 1909 by Dr Ing. E.H. Johann Schütte, was offering strong competition. Dr Schütte, a trained naval architect and engineer, was backed by two of Germany's top industrialists, Dr Karl Lanz and August Röchling. Schütte's designs were far in advance of von Zeppelin's but they suffered greatly through his choice of materials. He favoured a type of plywood held together with casein glue for the girders that made up the framework. This was chosen for the greatest possible lightness, but the wood was found to suffer badly from dampness and humidity, causing the framework to soften, come loose and ultimately fall apart.

The company manufactured twenty airships in all, eleven for the army and nine for the navy. Their vulnerability became apparent when the army lost nearly all their airships during the early part of the First World War from either ground fire or structural disintegration. The navy fared little better and turned to Count von Zeppelin for their airships.

In Britain aviation pioneers were not being idle. In 1902, just outside London, a small balloon-maker and aeronaut by the name of Stanley Spencer built a small non-rigid airship. It was 75ft long with a diameter of 20ft and was powered by a 3hp, water-cooled Sims engine that turned a 10ft-diameter propeller. Its first flight was from the grounds of Crystal Palace and, although slightly erratic in its course, it landed safely some 100 minutes after take-off. Spencer, at the same time as being an innovator, was also a businessman and hired his airships out for advertising purposes. The Evening News and Bovril companies were among those who used this very early form of aerial advertising.

Meanwhile, in Cardiff, Wales, another pioneer – a young man by the name of E.T. Willows – was building his own semi-rigid airship. Backed by his father and another failed airship builder, Captain William Beadle, he set to work to build his own airship, the Willows No.1. The airship was 74ft in length and had a diameter of 18ft, with a gas capacity of 12,000 cubic feet. It was powered by a 7hp Peugeot motorcycle engine which drove a 10ft-diameter propeller. This in turn rotated two airscrews at the end of the keel at half the speed of the main propeller. The two steering propellers were the invention of Capt. Beadle and were designed to swivel in the nose of the triangular keel. Willows continued to build airships and on 4 November 1910 the Willows No.2 made the first crossing of the English Channel to France. He progressed on to No.3 and No.4, both of which were examined in great detail by the RFC for possible operational use, but were rejected.

The British Army airship Dirigible No.1 made its appearance on 10 September 1907 at Farnborough. The Balloon Section at Farnborough, under the command of balloon enthusiast Colonel J.E. Capper, unofficially named her *Nulli Secundus*. She was 122ft in length and 26ft in diameter, of the non-rigid type, with a framework slung below the envelope to which was attached a small car that carried the engine and the crew. Power was provided by a French engine, the 50hp Antoinette. The first trials were extremely successful and caused great excitement in London when the airship appeared flying over St Paul's cathedral. The following year, the airship was redesigned in a semi-rigid construction which altered its shape. A triangular keel was fitted, making the ends of the airship pointed, and the hydrogen gas capacity was increased to 56,000 cubic feet. *Nulli Secundus* flew again on 14 July 1908 for the last time.

The British airship R.33, moored to her mast at Cardington.

An interesting shot of R.33 at Cardington. Note the construction of the cabin glass, affording the pilot an all-round view.

A second army dirigible, *Beta*, was under construction at the time of the demise of the *Nulli Secundus*. She was considerably smaller, being 84ft long and 24ft 8in in diameter with a gas capacity of 22,000 cubic feet. After a number of trials it was decided that the dirigible was too short for practical purposes and it was lengthened. One year later, on 10 May 1910, *Beta* reappeared, 20ft longer, with a gas capacity of 33,000 cubic feet and powered by a 35hp Green engine. Just before this, in February 1910, a third army dirigible made its appearance. This ship, the *Gamma*, was twice the size of *Beta*, with a gas capacity of 72,000 cubic feet and a 100hp Green Engine. To facilitate descent and landing the *Gamma*'s propellers were designed to swivel. Together with conventional tail fins, they made this dirigible one of the most stable platforms in the air.

Vickers at Barrow-in-Furness had also been involved in the construction of an airship, this one destined for the Royal Navy. HMA No.1, *Mayfly* as she was called, had been built at the beginning of May 1911. Mooring trials were carried out on 22 May 1911 and it was soon discovered that she carried too much weight for her frame. (The navy had insisted that the airship carry anchors and chains.) She was taken back into the hangar for numerous modifications to be made to her framework. On 24 September 1911 she was pulled out of her hangar stern-first for her first flight. Unfortunately, the unskilled naval handling party were caught unawares by a sudden gust of very strong wind and the airship struck the side of the hangar violently. The impact broke the *Mayfly*'s back and she was damaged beyond economical repair. She was scrapped without ever taking to the air. However, on the 18 July 1912 the Royal Navy purchased Willows No.4 and its hangar for £1,050, renaming it HMA No.2.

In Italy, the airship was beginning to waken the interest of the Italian military hierarchy. The first airship built appeared in 1909 and was called *Italia I*. It had been designed and built by Count Almerigo da Schio entirely at his own expense and resembled the British airship *Gamma*, with aerofoils, rudders and elevators that enabled it to be controlled to a great extent. A number of airships were built during the First World War and a number of sorties carried out, but the Italian use of airships was on nothing like the scale of that carried out by the British and Germans.

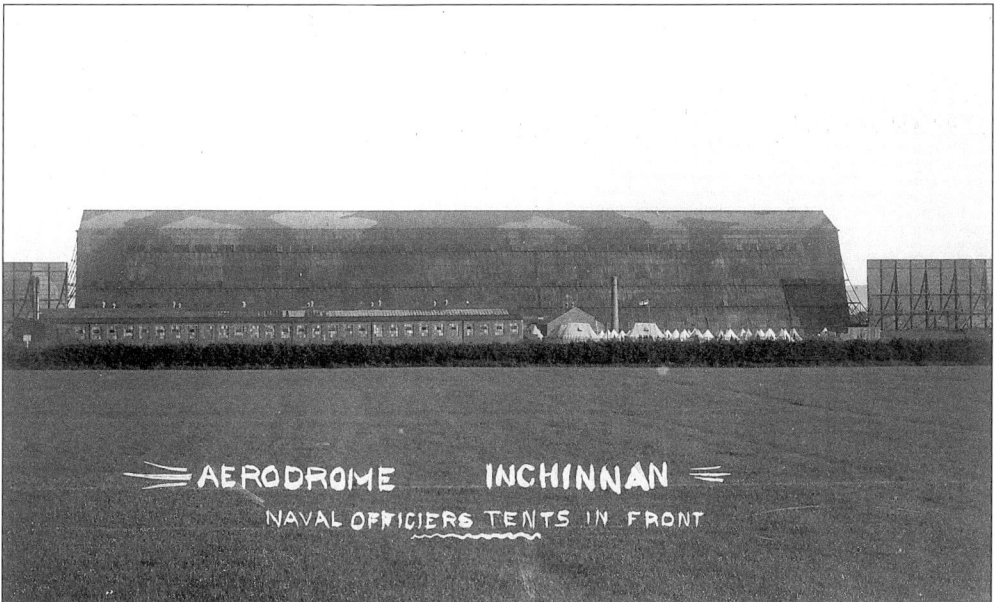

The giant airship shed at Royal Naval Air Station Inchinnan, Scotland, dwarfs the officers' tents in front of it.

The outbreak of the First World War awakened the flagging interest in airships in Britain. Captain Murray Sueter, RN, an ardent supporter of the airship, persuaded the government to place an order for a non-rigid airship and contacted a Mr Holt Thomas with regard to purchasing a French built airship, the *Astra-Torres*. Constructed in a tri-lobe configuration, the design allowed for an internal rigging system that allowed the loads within the envelope to be distributed more effectively. The design was accepted by the British and the airship flown to Farnborough.

Sueter later contacted a relatively unknown Berlin manufacturer of airships, Major Parseval, who had designed an airship that consisted of two balloons, one slightly larger than the other. The balloons were situated fore and aft, the smaller one to the fore and the larger just aft of midships. By transferring air from one to the other, it was possible to obtain a measure of fore and aft control, although in practice it was very slow to respond. The airship was 279ft long, with a diameter of 47ft8in and a gas capacity of 300,000 cubic feet. Powered by two 170hp Maybach engines, *Parseval* was able to reach a speed of 46mph. The airship was demonstrated by a Captain von Stelling, Parseval's chief pilot, then flown to Farnborough to join *Astra-Torres*.

Germany continued to lead the way with airship development, with France slowly falling back and concentrating mainly on aircraft development. The British, however, started to catch up, concentrating their wartime efforts on smaller airships that could be used for observation and convoy protection duties. But they did not completely ignore the development of the larger rigid airships. Sueter had been sent to Italy to evaluate a semi-rigid airship designed and built by Forlanini. There were a couple of other airship manufacturers in Italy at the time, but Forlanini's was the only one worth considering. However, after extensive tests and demonstrations, Sueter decided that the craft was extremely difficult to handle and very unreliable.

With the advent of war, the airship came into its own with regard to convoy protection. It was able to fly above convoys and keep pace with them while all the time scouring the surface of the sea for the telltale signs of a prowling submarine. The first of these airships

The R.23 built in 1917 by Vickers Ltd and powered by four 250hp Rolls Royce Eagle engines. The airship is seen here in 1918, carrying out trials of air-launching aircraft. Suspended beneath the fuselage of the airship is a Sopwith 2F1 Camel.

An aerial shot of the British R.26.

was the Willows No.4, with the fuselage of a BE.2c suspended beneath. This hybrid turned out to be an excellent prototype and a number were built based on the design. It became the forerunner of the SS (Sea Scout) types that eventually replaced it. The SS ships had an endurance of more than sixteen hours and a top speed of 40mph and carried a crew of two. This of course meant that they could fly way out into the Atlantic and meet the convoys, affording them some degree of protection.

Some sceptics held that, while the airship offered a great deal of protection to the convoy, it also highlighted its position to any enemy submarine that happened to be cruising on the surface some miles from the convoy itself. It was also argued that had the airship seen a submarine on the surface, its speed would not enable it to attack the submarine with any conviction. The fact is that no airship ever attacked a submarine while escorting a convoy and conversely no convoy was ever attacked while being escorted by an airship.

German submarine commanders feared the airship, mainly because they overestimated its actual ability to carry out an attack if it surprised a submarine on or just below the surface. They also realised that if spotted they could be tracked and the position passed to accompanying destroyers. The one thing that the airship could do that the seaplane could not, was to spot the thin film of oil that invariably escaped from the exhausts and hydroplanes of a submarine while it was below the surface. The film was so slight that only the slow-moving airship would have any chance of seeing the trace.

There were a variety of SS-types of airship: the SS Pusher, the SS Zero and the SS Twin. Some of these were replaced within two years by the 'C', or Coastal, type. These were based on the design of the *Astra-Torres* airship and were powered by two 180hp, eight-cylinder Sunbeam engines, one at each end of the gondola that was slung beneath. Twenty four of this type were built, each with a machine gun mounted on top of the envelope. As the war progressed, the usefulness of the 'C' type became more and more apparent, so a number of air stations started to spring up around the south and west coasts of England and Wales. RNAS Mullion in Cornwall was one of the main stations responsible for the protection of convoys that came up the Western Approaches. They patrolled the seas around them constantly, looking for faint traces of oil coming from the submarines and giving 'the Kaiser's tin fish' as the U-boats were nicknamed, no peace at all.

A larger version of the 'C' type was built, called the C* (C Star). It was twenty-five per cent larger with a cubic capacity of 200,000 cubic feet and was 218ft long with a width of 50ft and a height of 57ft. This was in turn superseded by the NS (North Sea) Class which had a cubic capacity of 360,000 cubic feet, was 262ft long and carried a crew of ten. The NS set the record for endurance under wartime conditions at sixty-one hours and twenty-one minutes. In 1919, this record was surpassed by one NS airship that stayed on patrol for just over 101 hours and covered some 4,000 miles.

The airship, from its unconvincing beginnings, proved its worth in the First World War. Although never given the same chances as those given to the aeroplane, she still managed to command the respect of all those she protected and all those who flew in her.

HM Airship C.10 coming into land at a snowbound RNAS Airship Station Longside, Aberdeen.

One
Germany

The first flight of the first Zeppelin.

The history of German airships can be contributed in essence to one man, Count Ferdinand von Zeppelin. Despite suffering early setbacks, von Zeppelin persevered with his construction of giant airships. The outbreak of the First World War brought new orders to von Zeppelin's recently formed company DELAG (Deutsche Luftschiffahrts-Aktien-Gesellschaft GmbH).

The first of the airships to be built by DELAG was the LZ.10, the *Schwaben*, in 1911 and despite teething troubles it made 218 flights before being destroyed in an accident on 28 June 1912. Then came orders from the military. The L.I was the first naval Zeppelin to be built, but crashed one year later in 1913, killing the head of the Naval Airship Division, Korvettenkapitän Friedrich Metzing. 'L' was the designation given to naval airships; thus the builder's number of L.1 was LZ.14. The LZ designation was retained by the army, which made it easy to identify whether or not an airship was army or navy. The second of the navy's airships was, naturally, L.2. This was destroyed after catching fire during altitude tests, killing all the crew.

Another airship construction company was slowly making inroads into the military market – the Luftschiffbau Schütte-Lanz company created by Dr Ing. E.H. Johann Schütte and backed by two Mannheim industrialists, Dr Karl Lanz and August Röchling. Their airships were not the success they had hoped for, mainly because of their choice of material (wood) in the construction of the airship's complicated framework.

Rapidly, the Germans discovered the vulnerability of the airship to ground fire and it was decided to use Zeppelins for night attacks or as scouting cruisers for the fleet. The first strategic raids were carried out on the night of 19-20 January 1915 by the L.3, L.4 and L.6. The damage they caused on this raid was more psychological than real. The huge, monstrous, elongated balloons seemed to fill the sky as they passed over houses on their way to bomb the so-called 'selected military targets'. The ordinary person in the street might have heard of such things but would rarely have seen them. It was the sheer size of the Zeppelins that was terrifying to those on the ground.

Further raids followed and one by L.10 on the South Shields area, on the night of the 15-16 June, caused considerable damage to factories on either side of the River Tyne. These raids from the air suddenly brought home to the people of Britain that wars were no longer being fought on distant battlefields but being carried right into their homes. The raids continued up to the end of 1916, when Korvettenkapitän Peter Strasser, now head of the Naval Airship Division, ordered all his airships to attack London repeatedly in an attempt to bring Britain to its knees. All Strasser managed to do was to see his fleet of airships almost entirely wiped out.

A new type of Zeppelin had been designed, known to the British as 'height-climbers'. These airships could carry out raids at heights of 16,000 to 20,000 feet, rendering the existing anti-aircraft guns obsolete. In retaliation to this new threat the RFC developed explosive bullet which, aided by a series of bad weather conditions and mechanical problems on the airships, spelled out the death knell for Zeppelin airships. The final raid on Britain was carried out on the night of 5-6 August 1918, by the L.53, L.46, L.65 and L.70. The four airships never reached their destination and Korvettenkapitän Peter Strasser, who led the flight in the L.70, was killed when his airship was shot down by incendiary bullets from a DH.4 No.A8032 flown by Majors Robert Leckie and Egbert Cadbury, RNAS. The L.53 was shot down by Lt S.D. Culley, RNAS, flying a Sopwith 2F1 Camel, before the remaining two airships turned around and headed back.

At the end of the war, the Zeppelin crews, still loyal to their country, destroyed five of the remaining Zeppelin airships in their shed at Nordholz and two more were destroyed at Wittmundhaven. The Zeppelins had not lived up to their expectations and crushed British resistance in Britain, but they left a legacy in aviation history.

The LZ.1 tethered to a barge on the evening of her maiden flight, when she was piloted by Count von Zeppelin himself.

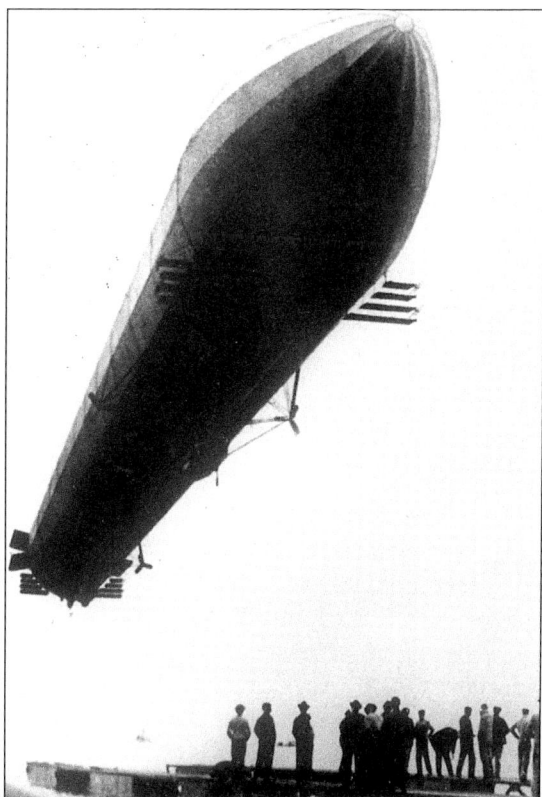

The first German naval Zeppelin, L.1, on her maiden flight.

Zeppelin L.1 being walked from her hangar.

SL.1 under construction, showing the gasbags within the framework.

Count Ferdinand von Zeppelin.

A front three-quarter view of Zeppelin L.1 taking off on a test flight.

Zeppelins *Victoria Luise* and *Sachsen*.

The Zeppelin L.2. This was the second rigid airship sold to the German Imperial Navy and is seen here just after catching fire. Seconds after this photograph was taken, the airship exploded.

Wreckage of the Zeppelin L.3 on the Danish island of Faroe after her engines failed.

The SL.2 (Luftschiffbau Schütte-Lanz), built for the German Army, is seen here on a test flight. She had a gas volume of 861,900 cubic feet contained in fifteen separate gasbags, a length of 474ft and a diameter of 59.7ft. Power was provided by four 95hp Maybach C-X engines.

The crew of the Zeppelin L.5 with their commander, Kapitänleutnant der Reserve Alois Böcker (front row, second from left).

Zeppelin L.11 in low flight. This ship raided Harwich on 2 September 1916.

After being damaged by British gunfire, the Zeppelin L.12 managed to struggle back across the English Channel and ditch in the sea just off Ostend. She is seen here being towed into Ostend by a German ship.

Following page: The burnt-out remains of a London bus that was hit by bombs dropped from the German airship L.15. The bus was hit during an attack on London's theatreland on 13 October 1915. The driver, the conductor and two passengers were killed.

The L.20, seen here in 1916, wrecked off the Norwegian coast near Stavanger after running out of fuel, was one of eight raiders that attempted to attack the British mainland. It was captained by Kapitänleutnant Stabbert.

Kapitänleutnant Robert Koch in the control car of his airship, the L.24. Koch took part in a number of bombing raids in this airship, including the one on Hull when twenty-one people were killed or injured. He and his new airship, the L.39, were destroyed on 17 March 1917 when they were shot down by anti-aircraft fire over Compiègne, France.

Airship commanders. Clockwise from top left: Kapitänleutnants Alois Böcker of the L.14, Peter Strasser of the L.70, Heinrich Mathay of the L.31 and Joachim Breithaupt of the L.15.

Zeppelin L.21 inside her shed at Nordholz in 1916. She was shot down in September 1917 after having carried out twelve raids and seventy flights.

The L.30 (LZ.62), the first of the 'R' types. She had a gas volume of 1,949,600 cubic feet contained in nineteen separate gasbags, was 649.5ft in length, had a diameter of 78.4ft and was powered by six Maybach HSLu engines.

The remains of a crashed Zeppelin that just made it over the border into Germany.

Members of the RFC carrying the coffins of the crew of the German airship SL.11 on 8 September 1916. This burial caused quite a stir at the time, as feelings ran high about the deaths of children that resulted from the raid by the SL.11. One woman is said to have thrown eggs at the coffins as they were carried into the cemetery.

A shot of the Zeppelin L.31 taken from inside the Normann shed at Nordholz. The knotted ropes in the foreground and the tail that can be seen to the right of the L.31 belong to the L.30.

The L.31 being walked into her shed at Nordholz.

Army Zeppelin LZ.37 being guided gently into her shed at Cologne.

Flt Sub Lt Rex Warneford's Morane-Parasol in which he shot down the German Zeppelin LZ.37.

The giant revolving shed *Nobel* at Nordholz. The shed weighed 4000 tons and was 652ft long.

The crew of the Zeppelin LZ.38. This was the first airship crew to bomb London.

Soon after returning from bombing London, the LZ.38 and its shed at Evére, near Brussels, were attacked by two British aircraft and destroyed. The shed is seen here blazing furiously with the remains of the LZ.38 inside.

The burnt-out shed at Evére after being bombed by British aircraft, with the remains of the LZ.38 smouldering inside.

Kapitänleutnant Franz Stabbert of the L.44 (left) and Kapitänleutnant Joachim Breithaupt of the L.15.

German Naval airship L.48. This Zeppelin was shot down in flames by Captain Saundby and Lt Watkins on 17 June 1917 while on a bombing raid over Theberton, Suffolk.

Zeppelin commanders. From left to right: Hauptmann Kuno Manger (L.62), Kapitänleutnant der Reserve Franz Georg Eicher (L.48), Kapitänleutnant Hans-Karl Gayer (L.49).

Zeppelin L.70, in which Körvettenkapitän Peter Strasser was shot down and killed on 5 August 1918 by Majors Egbert Cadbury and Robert Leckie in their DH4 No.A8032.

From left to right: Major Robert Leckie, -?-, Major Egbert Cadbury.

An unidentified German Zeppelin starting out on a mission. The tranquillity shown in this photograph belies the terror the Zeppelins brought to Britain's cities.

Looking like a giant monster from outer space, the SL.5 is seen here coming apart after being subjected to violent winds.

L.71 (LZ.113) had a gas volume of 2,418,700 cubic feet, a length of 743.17ft and a diameter of 78.4ft. She made her maiden flight on 29 July 1918 but was decommissioned after just eight flights.

Zeppelin L.46 in flight over Germany. This was a 'T'-type airship with a volume of 1,970,300 cubic feet and was the first to have streamlined cars amidships. She and the L.47, L.51, L.58 and SL.20 were destroyed in a mysterious fire in their sheds at Ahlhorn on 5 January 1918. The cause was never discovered.

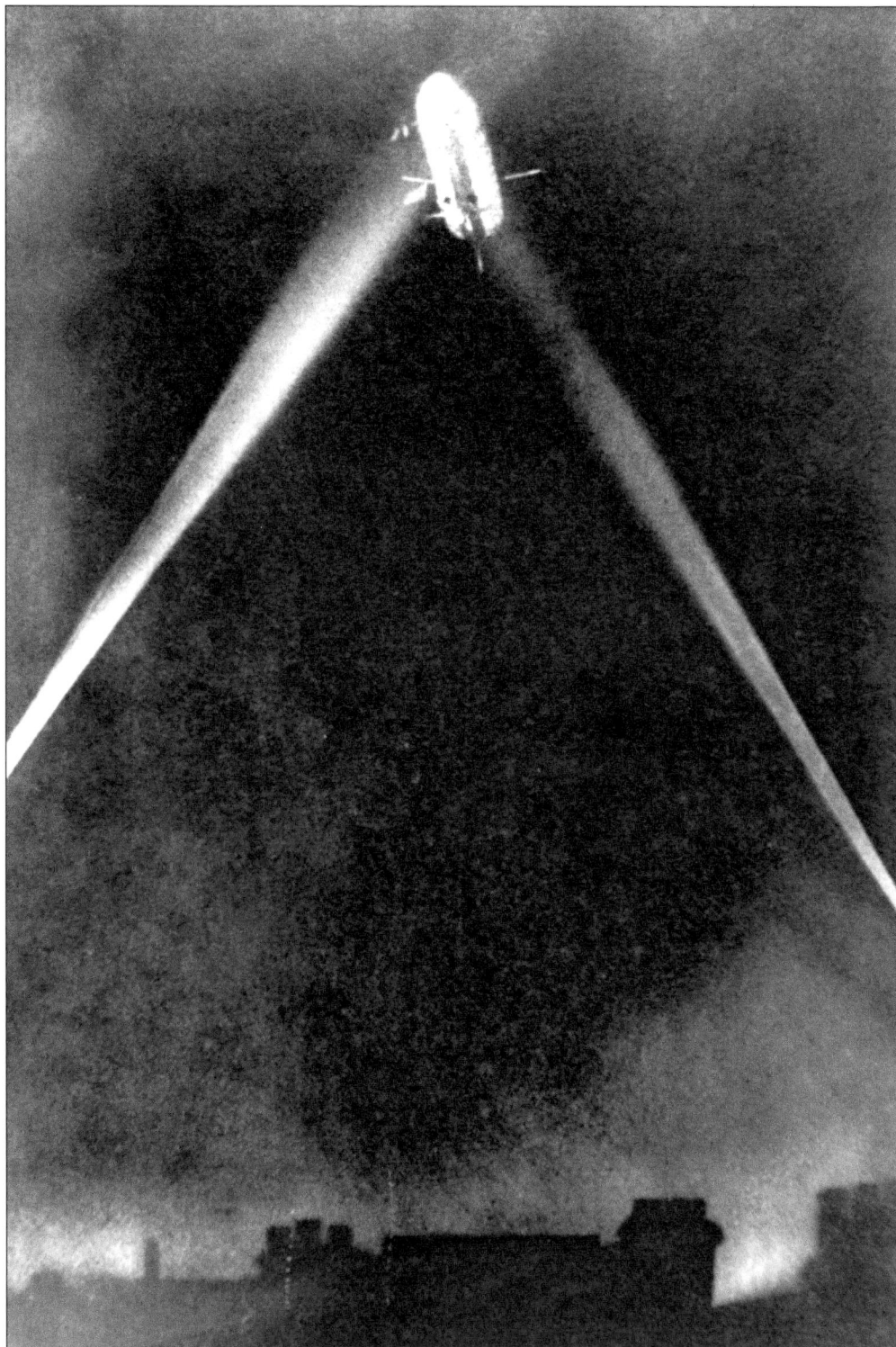

A German Zeppelin caught in the searchlights during a raid on London.

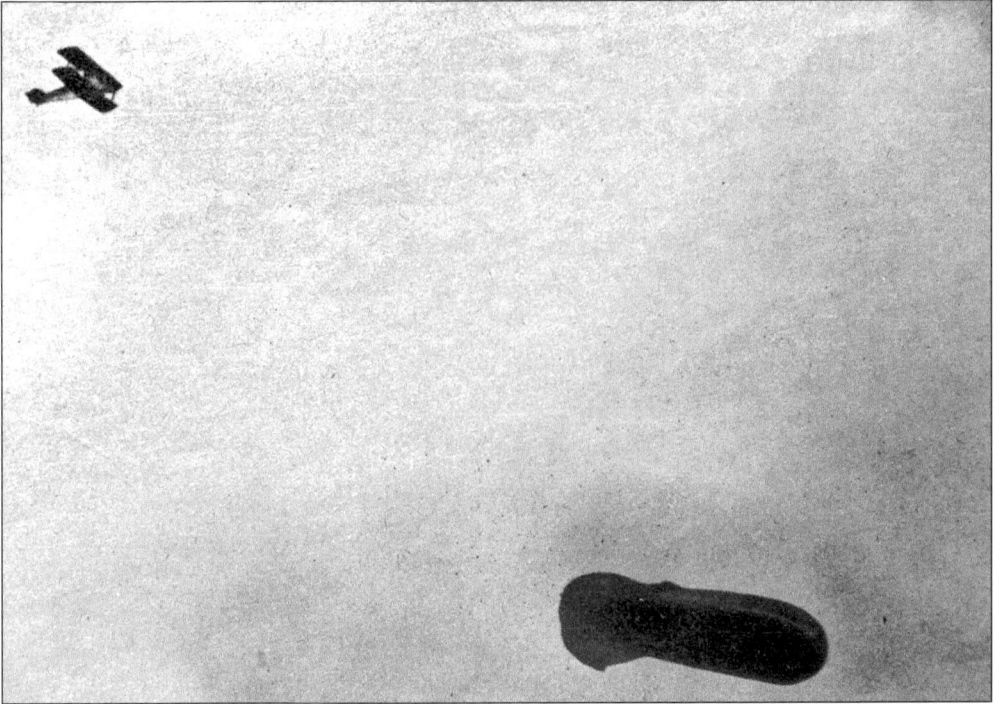

Allied aircraft about to attack a German Drachen observation balloon.

A German observer parachuting to safety after his observation balloon had been hit.

A Drachen observation balloon plunging to the ground after being attacked by British fighters.

The wreckage of the Zeppelin LZ.77, still burning after crashing in France.

A selection of bombs carried by the German naval Zeppelins. The large bomb with the crewman standing beside it is a 660lb explosive bomb. The others, in descending order of size, are 220lb, 110lb and 22lb. A pair of incendiaries is shown at either side of the cart.

Bomb damage to the sitting room of a house in Wallsend after a bombing raid by Zeppelins.

Zeppelins caused this damage to a bedroom in Wallsend.

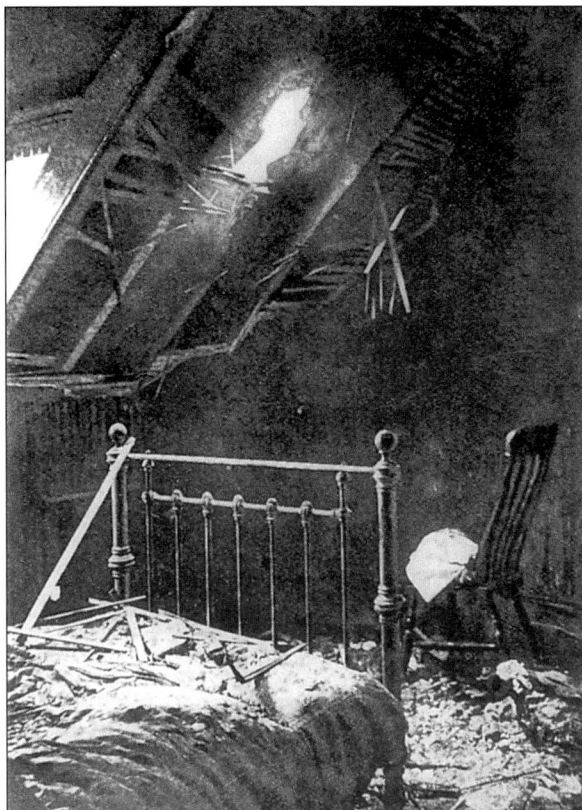

The remains of three German bombs recovered from a bomb-damaged house after a Zeppelin raid in Wallsend.

A series of scenes showing the aftermath of a Zeppelin raid on Colchester, Essex, on 21 February 1915.

Searchlights catch a German Zeppelin in their beams over London.

A German Zeppelin flying over a battleship of the German Grand Fleet at the Battle of Jutland.

Zeppelin L.33 overflies a German battleship at Jutland.

A view of Heligoland naval station, taken from a Zeppelin. The newly constructed seaplane dock is in the foreground.

An aerial shot of the German naval airship base at Wittmundhaven.

An aerial shot of Nordholz naval airship station. In the foreground are the giant sheds *Nogat* and *Nordstern*. On the far left end can be seen the revolving shed *Nobel* while in the middle distance is the shed *Normann*.

A Zeppelin hangar ablaze at Tondern after being bombed by RNAS aircraft.

Avro 504 No.179 being prepared for take-off at Belfort, France, on 21 November 1914. This aircraft was one of four that was to attack the Zeppelin sheds at Friedrichshafen. No.179, flown by Flt Sub Lt Cannon, broke a tail skid on take-off and was scratched from the raid.

The pilot of a Sopwith Camel being rescued after ditching close to the lighter from which he had taken off. This was precisely the situation Lt Culley was faced with when he returned to his lighter after attacking Zeppelin L.53.

An RNAS Pemberton Billing aircraft alongside the wreckage of a Zeppelin, possibly the L.33.

The commander of the LZ.37, Oberleutnant Otto von der Haegen (fourth from left), in the car of Zeppelin Ersatz EZ.1.

The imprint left in the ground by a luckless crewman of a Zeppelin after he fell to his death when his airship was destroyed by ground fire.

Previous page: Devastation in the Croydon area after the German Zeppelin L.14 had dropped her bombs on a 'military target'.

Two
Britain

An observation balloon at the Bristol Flying School.

In January 1914 the War Office decided that the newly constituted Royal Naval Air Service (RNAS) would take on charge the British Army's small fleet of non-rigid airships. When the First World War broke out in August 1914, the RNAS had just seven non-rigid operational airships. With the German U-boat menace threatening British shipping, the Admiralty boldly ordered an urgent procurement programme to combat the U-boats by aerial patrols of airships. This programme resulted in the production of SS-1 Sea Scout Class airships, which first flew in March 1915. The SS Class consisted of a lifting envelope with a BE.2 aircraft – minus wings and tailplane – suspended beneath. Other fuselages used were the FK.3 and Maurice Farmans. With a crew of two – pilot and observer-W/T operator – the airship could carry a bomb load of up to 112lb.

The Admiralty soon realised that there was a need for larger airships with a longer range. This resulted in the development of the Coastal Class airship, which came into use in May 1915. The C.1 airship was 196ft long with two engines, one pusher and one tractor. Its armament consisted of two Lewis machine guns and four 112lb or two 230lb bombs or depth charges. Its range depended on the weather, but it had a maximum speed of 47mph with an endurance of some twenty hours.

The next airship class to be developed was the Coastal Star (C*), longer than the Coastal Class and with many modifications – including provision for parachutes for the five-man crew. Ten Coastal Star airships were produced and were highly successful on operations. During 1916 the Admiralty issued another airship specification. This was for a 262ft-long, non-rigid airship – the North Sea Class. The first North Sea Class airship, NS.1, flew on 1 February 1917 at RNAS Kingsnorth. Probably the most comfortable of British airships so far, it had a tapered, fully enclosed, 35ft-long control cabin with provision for the ten-man crew to work, eat and sleep during a 24-hour flight. Armament was between three and five Lewis machine guns and six 230lb bombs. Eighteen North Sea airships were built but only sixteen became operational, the last three, NS.15, NS.17 and NS.18, were completed but never flown due to the end of the war.

1916 also saw the appearance of the Sea Scout Pusher, SSP Class airship, intended to replace the earlier SS Class. The Sea Scout Pusher, so named because it had a rear-mounted pusher-type engine, had a comfortable control cabin for its three-man crew of pilot, W/T operator and engineer. Six SSPs were built, of which three, Nos 1, 5 and 6, survived until the Armistice; Nos 2 and 4 were lost on operations at sea and No.3 was wrecked on her first flight.

Another airship class, the 143ft-long Sea Scout Zero Class, was developed at Capel. This airship had a streamlined, aluminium-covered, watertight control car for a three-man crew: pilot, wireless operator/gunner and engineer. It was powered by a new, water-cooled, 75hp Rolls Royce Hawk engine, which gave a better performance at the low speeds suited to an airship. Seventy-seven SSZs were built and they proved to be excellent operational airships. Operational development continued with three experimental, twin-engine, non-rigid airships, the SS Experimental (SSE) Class, being built and flown. The class was not proceeded with but the Sea Scout Twin (SST) Class was developed from it. Interestingly, the numbering of the SSTs excluded number 13, the numbers being 1 to 12 and 14.

Although the First World War was drawing to a close the Admiralty was still looking at airship usage and became interested in the Italian M Class semi-rigid airships. In July 1918 an M Class was bought from Italy and after tests was flown to England. The semi-rigid, now known by its British classification SR-1, carried a normal crew of eight but could carry more if needed. The only mission of the SR-1 was on 20 November 1918 when she escorted a British destroyer flotilla that was escorting a surrendered German submarine to Harwich.

The Admiralty did not see any use for large rigid airships during the war, preferring the smaller non-rigids. However, eighteen rigid craft were built and designated HMA – His Majesty's Airship. (HMA No.1 was, of course, the Mayfly of 1911.) The only success recorded by HMAs was by HMA R.29, which engaged three German U-boats on 29 September 1918. UB-115 was disabled with a 220lb bomb and sunk by surface destroyers.

During the First World War, the British Airship Branch suffered 234 casualties: fifty-four men were killed, 175 injured and five missing. Another five were interned for the duration of the war.

Nulli Secundus on a training flight. This was the first of the airships to be built at Farnborough.

The airship *Gamma* leaving her shed at Aldershot in 1910.

HM Airship *Gamma*, moored while being prepared for a test flight.

His Majesty's Airships *Baby* and *Beta*.

Beta in flight.

HMA *Delta* moored with *Beta* in the background.

HMA No.1 *Mayfly* lying with her back broken after an accident occurred while she was being removed from her floating shed at Cavendish Dock, Barrow, on 24 September 1911.

Following page: A close-up of the two-seat gondola of the SSZ.29 (Sea Scout Zero) non-rigid naval airship, showing its bombs, Lewis machine-gun and ballast bags.

A starboard-side view of the SSZ.1's gondola.

SSZ.59 aboard HMS *Furious*. SSZ.60 flies overhead.

The car of airship SSZ.71 at Kingsnorth in 1918.

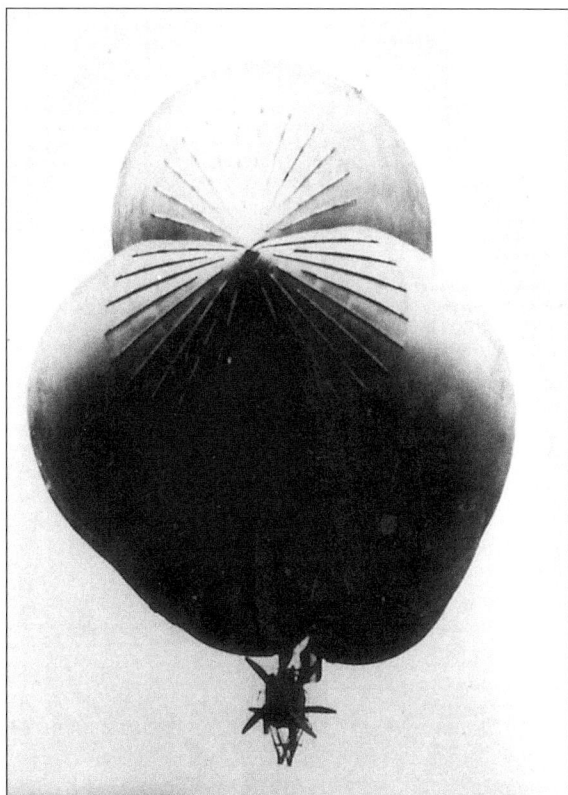

A head-on shot of a Coastal Class airship, showing perfectly the tri-lobe envelope.

Ladies preparing 'goldbeater's skin' (part of the large intestine of cattle) for lining gas cells. More than a million skins would be required for a large airship.

The goldbeater's skin is stuck to cotton panels prior to being fitted into the cheese shape of the envelope panels. In the background one of the completed cells is being inflated for leak tests.

The SS.2 (formerly Willows) airship after being heavily modified for the RNAS. It is seen here at Dover on 9 April 1915.

SSZ.20 being prepared for patrol at Luce Bay in 1918.

A C Star airship in low-level flight.

The wreckage of the SS.10 after coming down in the English Channel on 10 September 1915. The rowing boat is bringing a towline to the trawler in the foreground.

SSZ.17 is hauled down by her handling crew at Pembroke in 1917.

SSZ.19 approaching its landing site at Polegate, 1917.

The SST.1 (Submarine Scout Twin) being prepared for take-off. Powered by two 75hp Rolls Royce engines mounted on struts above the four-seat car, the airship was 165ft long with a diameter of 35ft and a volume of 100,900 cubic feet.

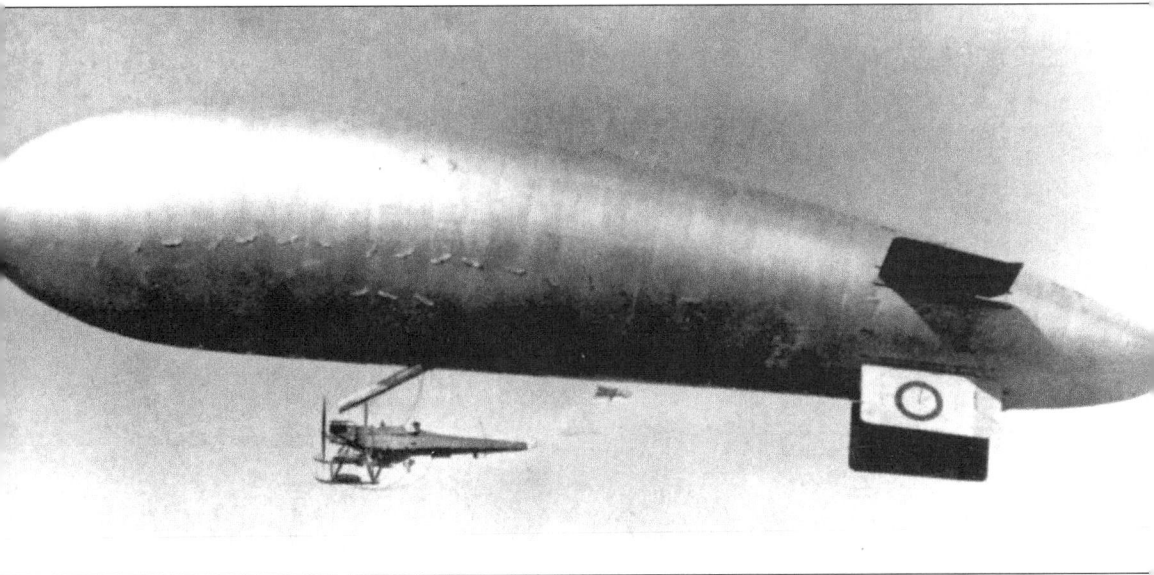
SSBE 19. This was the only airship of its type to serve in the Aegean.

An SSZ airship being walked into its hangar by an all-women ground handling crew at Howden.

Sea Scout airship SSZ.11 being readied for launch.

SS airships on patrol in the English Channel. The airship in the foreground had been towed into position by the ship in order to increase its range. The towing line can just be seen to the right of the photograph.

Tranquillity. Although this SSZ airship was on patrol over the North Sea during the First World War, the scene is one of pure serenity.

SSZ.3 coming in to land after being on patrol.

An aerial shot of RNAS Luce Bay, Stranraer, Scotland. Note the protective wind screens at either end of the shed.

The BE.2 fuselage that was used on the early types of SS airships. This one is from SS.10. Note the anchor hanging from beneath the fuselage. This picture highlights the precarious situation in which the crew had to operate.

The SSZ.47 being deflated at a mooring site near Mullion Air Station.

The crew of the SSZ.26 being rescued from their sinking craft after it ditched into the sea. The airship was from the RNAS station at Polegate in Sussex and was photographed from a sister airship.

The SSZ.53 being inflated in its shed at Pembroke in 1918.

Airship C.27 makes an emergency landing after engine failure.

The captain of the airship C.18 climbing aboard his craft prior to launch.

The wreckage of the C.16, which crashed at Coldingham Bay near Berwick on 28 August 1916 after both engines failed.

The airship C.14 being prepared for launch at Longside in 1914. Note the fuselage-mounted Lewis gun in its stowed position.

A C Class airship being handled in strong winds, as evidenced by the number of ground handlers required to maintain control.

HM Airship C.4 at RNAS Airship Station Longside, taking off to go on patrol over the North Sea.

Following page: HM Airship C.10A in her hangar at RNAS Station Longside, Aberdeen, about to be brought out by handlers who can just be seen beneath the fuselage.

C*6 on patrol off the Cornish coast on 5 June 1918, watching over a fleet of trawlers.

Airship C*8, decorated for the Armistice celebrations.

C*9 being prepared for flight at RNAS Howden.

The airship C.12 in her hangar at Polegate in October 1916. In the background is the SS.16.

The wreckage of NS.2 at Stoneham – near Stowmarket – on 27 June 1917.

Opposite (top): HMA (His Majesty's Airship) No.5, one of the British-built Parsevals, showing the enclosed cabin.
Opposite (bottom): A front three-quarter view of an NS (North Sea) airship with its handling party. The enclosed cabin and the tri-lobe envelope can be clearly seen.

The modified car of the NS.3 showing the 'bumping' bags' mounted beneath.

The crew of the North Sea 3.

% William Walter Warner (cox)
died 1923 aged 38

Coastal airship on patrol over the North Sea.

A balloon 'apron' over London in 1914. The idea was good but in practice the system proved totally unsatisfactory.

British officers about to go aloft in their observation balloon.

A British observation balloon being manhandled into a new position in 1916 – sometimes a difficult and laborious task.

A British balloon observer descending on his parachute.

Two artillery officers at Gosnay on 2 May 1918, preparing to go aloft in a balloon.

A British observer hooked up by his parachute in a tree after leaping clear of his observation balloon.

Following page: Officers of No.3 Balloon Section, Kite Balloon Service, RNAS, early in 1915. Left to right, back row: Flt Sub Lt O.A.Butcher, Flt Sub Lt D. Gill, Flt Sub Lt R.A. Davey, Flt Sub Lt G.G. Omanney. Seated: Flt Sub Lt P.C. Douglas, Lt B.S. Benning, Colonel E.M. Maitland, Sub-Lt C. Windeler and Sub-Lt H.F. Mills.

The SR.1 about to land at Pulham. Note the two sleeping berths fixed to the envelope in front of the car. One wonders how the crew managed to get in and out of these precariously fixed berths.

The R.9 airship at Pulham on 30 May 1918 with her outer skin removed showing the gasbags.

R.9 being walked out of her shed at Howden on 5 April 1917.

A fine front three-quarter view of R.23. Note the converted tank that is being used as a mooring platform in front of the airship.

Sopwith 2F1 Camel No.N6814 suspended beneath the fuselage of HMA 23 at Pulham in 1918. Trials of air-launching aircraft to extend their range were being carried out. The pilot was Lt R.E.Keys of No.212 Squadron, RAF.

A rare photograph of the moment at which Lt Keys' Sopwith Camel detached from HMA 23.

R.25 approaching the handling party in preparation for landing.

The R.26 airship in a nose down attitude about to be hauled down by the handling party.

Airship R.9 near the ground. This was the first British rigid dirigible to fly.

Previous page: R.24 moored to her mast at Cardington with all her handling lines hanging down ready for operation. When this photograph was taken – on 16 July 1919 – the R.24 had been moored at mast for six days in heavy rain, thunderstorms and winds gusting up to 50mph.

R.26 being hauled down at Cardington.

R.24 at East Fortune on 8 December 1917.

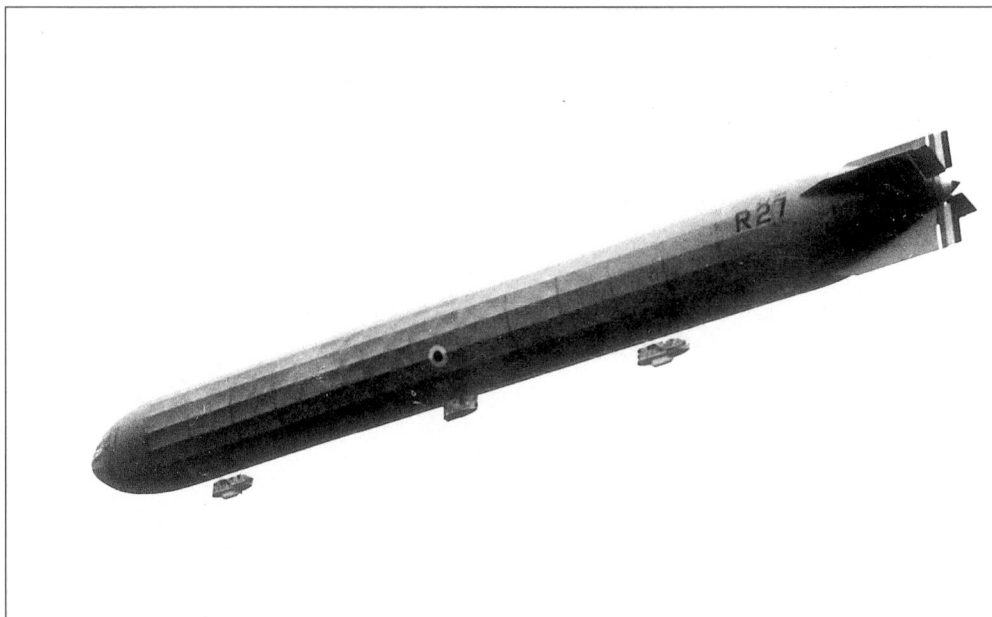

An aerial shot of the R.27 going on patrol.

R.31 being prepared for lift-off with ground handling crew spread along her length.

The R.33 being walked out of her shed at Vickers. All the ground handling crew are civilians.

The tail turret on the R.33, highlighting the precarious situation of the tail gunner. The turret was later removed.

R.33 at her mooring mast.

A head-on view of R.31 coming in to land.

R.34 just lifting off from Cardington.

R.36, mast-moored at Cardington.

A C Type blimp moored to a yoke-style mooring mast in its hangar.

HMA 23 coming in to land at a very sharp angle.

Three

France

An engraving of the Battle of Fleurus, when balloon observation aided a French victory.

The French contribution to the world of military aeronautics can be traced back to the Franco-Prussian War of 1794. Two companies of *aérostiers* were formed under the collective name of the Military Aerostatic Company and the command of Captain Coutelle. Their first incursion into war was when Captain Coutelle took his balloon, *L'Entreprenant*, to Maubeuge and carried out a flight to observe the disposition of the Dutch and Austrian troops. His observations allowed the French artillery to lay down a number of extremely accurate artillery barrages, causing horrendous casualties among the opposing troops.

One month later Coutelle ascended to the skies again, this time over Fleurus, where he stayed aloft for over ten hours passing information, by means of notes attached to weighted cords, to the French artillery. Because of his significant part in these successful actions, Napoleon promoted him to General and gave him command of the Balloon Corps, which by then consisted of four companies. Unfortunately, after suffering a severe defeat by the British in Egypt in 1799, the Corps was disbanded because of its inability to be mobile.

A number of balloon flights, both military and civil, precipitated the arrival of the airship. The French government established an aeronautical establishment at Chalais-Meudon in the 1880s and it was from there that *La France* made its first historic flight in 1884. The airship had been financed by Léon Gambetta, who had escaped from Paris during the siege of 1870 by balloon, and was built by two army engineers, Charles Renard and Arthur Krebs. It wasn't until 1903, however, that Alberto Santos-Dumont, a Brazilian who had been constructing airships in France since 1898, demonstrated his No.9 airship to the military. They were impressed and appointed Commandant Hirschauer, Chief of the Battalion of Balloonists, and Lt Col. Bouttiaux to examine in detail the military potential of the airship.

Even so it was only just before the outbreak of the First World War that France began to look seriously at the use of airships in the military. One of the companies that did so was the Société Astra des Constructions Aéronautiques. They took over the designs of Torres Quevedo and improved on them, producing the Astra-Torres airships. These airships had a trefoil-shaped (tri-lobed) envelope and incorporated the rigging within the airship, which lowered the wind resistance when in flight. During the First World War, nearly all the Astra-Torres airships were used by the French Naval Air Service for patrol duties in the Mediterranean. Five of these airships, AT.2, AT.3, AT.6, AT.7 and AT.8, were sent to North Africa to patrol the waters there.

Another airship factory, the state owned factory at Chalais-Meudon, built a total of eleven airships for the army (seven) and navy (four) during the First World War. The first four – CM.1, CM.2, CM.3 and CM.4 – built for the navy were based in the Western Approaches and served with distinction throughout the war. Four more of these airship were proposed but never delivered.

Two other airship constructors came to the fore just before the outbreak of the war, the Société Zodiac and the Clement-Bayard Factories. Société Zodiac constructed a number of airships, among them two training airships, the Cruiser-class *Captain Ferber* and Scout-class *Le Temps*, (named after the newspaper that collected from its readers the money for its construction), as well as the *Champagne* and *D'Arlandes*. The Clement-Bayard factory constructed the *Clement-Bayard I*, *Clement-Bayard II*, *Depuy de Lôme* and *Adjudant Vincenot*.

It became increasingly obvious that the intense anti-aircraft fire that was used against the airships was taking its toll. They did not have the speed or manoeuvrability to evade the intense barrages and so it was decided that their future lay with the navy, hunting for U-boats and protecting convoys. In March 1917 all French airships and their crews, were handed over to the control of the navy and by the end of the war the French airship, like its British counterpart, had distinguished itself and proved its sceptics wrong.

A drawing of the very first aerial flight, made by a hot-air balloon in 1783.

A fantasy drawing, *Le Cheval Aéronaute*, showing a rider and his horse being flown in a balloon.

Jules Durof's balloon about to take off from Montmartre during the siege of Paris in 1870.

The Brazilian airship designer and builder Santos-Dumont demonstrating one of his dirigibles.

Santos-Dumont standing in the car of one of his dirigibles.

The French airship *Champagne* at Toul in May 1916. Built by the Zodiac company, she was powered by two 220hp Zodiac engines. At the top of the airship can be seen the dorsal gun position. This was reached by the gunner climbing through a canvas tube that extended from the bottom to the top of the envelope.

The French naval airship AT.4, built by the Astra-Torres company. Powered by two 150hp Renault engines, she was 223ft long, with a diameter of 44.5ft and a gas volume of 229,515 cubic feet.

The French airship *Adjudant Vincenot*, built by the Clement-Bayard company for the French Army. She made thirty-four operational flights during the First World War.

The French airship *Le Temps*, built by the Zodiac company and used for training purposes.

The French airship *Général Meusnier*, built by the Clement-Bayard company, seen here carrying out trials at Issy in October 1915.

French balloon-airship officers at Toul in 1914. From left to right, standing: De Kergarrieu, Poux, Lieutenant de Voucoux, -?-, -?-, Captain Dinochau, Lieutenant Périsée de Bédé (*Adjudant Vincenot*), Captain Tixier (*Fleurus*), M. Julliot, Captain Delagsus (*Adjudant Réau*), Captain Joux (*Adjudant Vincenot*). Seated: De Vigerous d'Arvieu, Captain Néant, Captain Izaud (Station Commander), Lieutenant Pacquingone (*Adjudant Vincenot*), Depoux (M. Julliot's assistant).

The crew car of the French army airship *Alsace*, built by the Astra-Torres company from the parts of the scrapped airship *Pilâtre de Rozier*.

CBV.1, the sixth airship to be built by Clement-Bayard. She was sold to Russia in 1914.

France's only rigid airship, *Spiess*, built by the Zodiac Company. She had a gas volume of 579,084 cubic feet, was 370ft long and had a diameter of 44.5ft.

A Lebaudy airship bought by the Morning Post newspaper for the army. She made her first flight on 14 July 1910 and was destroyed on 4 May 1911 after crashing across the Farnborough road.

The French army airship *Fleurus I* at Reims, the first Allied airship to carry out a bombing raid. She had a gas volume of 370,755 cubic feet, a length of 305ft and a diameter of 46ft.

A French experimental airship in flight. The car suspended beneath the airship appears to be part of the fuselage of an aircraft as can be seen by the wheels at the front.

A French Cagout balloon being raised.

Four

Italy

An O.1 semi-rigid airship, also known as OS or Osservatore ship, seen here landing at Ciampino. Built by the Stabilimento di Construzioni Aeronautiche in 1918, she was used as a scout ship. She was 177.66ft long and 35.33ft in diameter with a gas volume of 123,700 cubic feet.

The first Italian contribution to LTA (Lighter Than Air) flight started back in the early 1800s. The first use for the military, however, was when the military balloon service was formed in 1884 and three years later used in the Eritrean Campaign of 1887-88. The service consisted of three balloons, which were used for observation and communication duties. During the four months of active service in which the balloons were used, over thirty ascents were made. They had proved their worth and it was just a process of natural progression to the airship.

The airship made its first appearance in 1905, when Count Almerigo da Schio built the airship *Italia I*, based closely on the design of the British airship *Gamma*, but it wasn't until 1911 that the first army airship made its appearance in manoeuvres. There were, at the time, two types available: the Forlanini and the 'P' type. The one selected by the military was the semi-rigid 'P' model. It was designed by Messrs Usuelli, Crocco and Munari and was 203.42ft long, had a cubic capacity of 176,500 cubic feet and was powered by two 70hp Fiat S54 engines, turning two four-bladed, variable-pitch propellers.

Airships were first used operationally against the Turks, P.1 and P.2 being based at Tripoli and Benghazi. They were used primarily to find and bomb the principal Turk and Arab bases and to intercept camel trains. During the campaign, both crews of the airships carried out numerous bombing and reconnaissance patrols, ending the war with the praises of the Commander-in-Chief of the Italian Army ringing in their ears.

At the beginning of the First World War, the Italian army had already accrued a great deal of experience using airships under wartime conditions. But it wasn't until the middle of 1915 that two additional types of airship, the M and the V, were built for both the army and the navy. The military had four airships at the beginning of the war and had established four bases, Venice and Verona for the army and Ferrara and Iesi for the navy. The first strike by these airships was when P.4 and P.5 attempted to attack the military base at Pola on the night of 25-26 May 1915. They were unsuccessful because of the strength of the military defence that surrounded the base. The following night the M class airships attacked the shipyards at San Marco and the Trieste-Nabresins railway and, despite poor conditions, were very successful. The loss of the M.4 at the beginning of 1916, whilst attacking Gorizia, was a great blow to the navy.

In 1917, the number of military airships had risen to nine, consisting of two bombers and seven scouts. During this year the number of raids increased and so did airship losses. On one night in April the M.3. was lost to ground fire while the M.10 suffered considerable damage but survived. Then, on 23 July, the M.2 was lost with all its crew. In one major incident in September 1917, three airships – M.1, M.10 and M.14 – attacked Proseccio. During the raid, the M.10 was hit and forced to leave the area. One of the officers, Lt. Castruccio climbed from the crew compartment into the envelope of the airship and lay down for one and a half hours at the mooring point in an attempt to keep the airship trimmed. For this act of bravery, he was awarded the *Medaglia d'Oro* (the Italian equivalent to the Victoria Cross). By the end of the war, army airships had carried out over 197 raids and dropped 133 tons of bombs. The navy had made over 1,300 scouting flights covering a total of 157,000 miles (252,563 km). Thirteen men had been killed, ten captured and twelve airships lost.

Left: A head-on view of the Italian semi-rigid airship M.6, showing the precarious position of the forward machine-gunner.
Right: The rear aspect gives a good view of the fragile control surfaces.

In the foreground is an A Class airship showing the distinctive shape of its envelope. The airship on the right of the picture is either an M- or a P- type.

The Italian semi-rigid airship P.4, built by the Stabilimento di Construzioni Aeronautiche for the Italian Army.

The prototype semi-rigid M.1 airship on trials. Built by the Stabilimento di Construzioni Aeronautiche, it had a gas volume of 441,375 cubic feet, was 271.25ft long and had a diameter of 55ft.

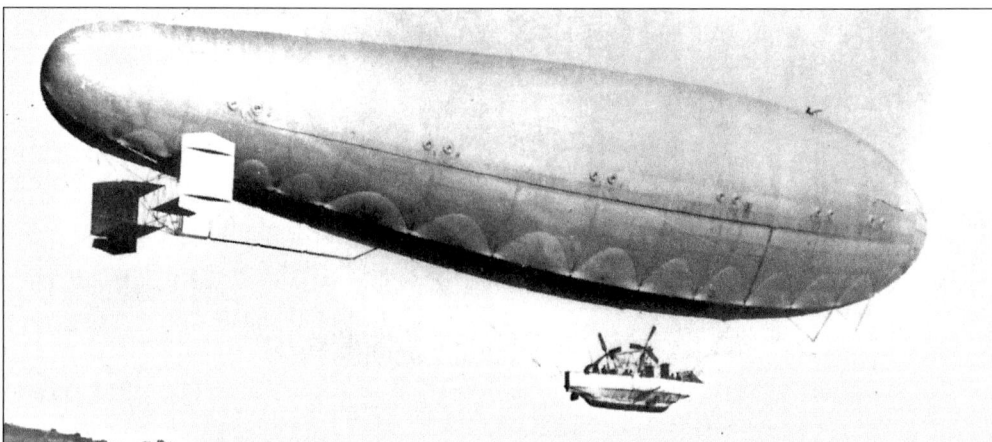

The M.6 coming in to land. The Italians built eighteen M Types (Medio), powered by twin Italia engines and capable of carry up to one ton of bombs.

The port side of the car of the M.6.

A starboard-side view of the M.6 car.

The Italian airship M.10 leaving her shed. Note the machine gun position on top of the envelope and the observation platform on top of the airship's shed.